The Vicissitudes of Life

From
Dusk
to
Dawn

HENRY KRAUSS

To order additional copies of this book, contact:
Xlibris
844-714-8691
www.Xlibris.com
Orders@Xlibris.com

ISBN: Softcover   978-1-6641-8353-7
        Hardcover   978-1-6641-8354-4
        EBook   978-1-6641-8352-0

Library of Congress Control Number: 2021913681

Print information available on the last page

Rev. date: 08/12/2021

Contents

JANUARY 5, 2021

Icicles

BY HENRY KRAUSS

It started
with just one
snowflake.
Then it began
to blow
into a storm.
It was frigid.
No visibility.
Whirling snow.
Huge drifts
Lightning flashed,
thunder roared.

Icicles hung
from the roofs.
They were
thick, sturdy.
They lasted
many days
in the freezing cold.

Gradually
the sun came out.
The icicles
began to drip
ever so slightly.
Finally
they began
to fall.
Melted.

Most of our lives
we are strong.
After the sun
beats down on us
over the years,
we weaken
and melt.

But
the water
evaporates
to heaven.
Our souls
last forever.

My Coffee Table

BY HENRY KRAUSS

I gaze at the table-small, round, little stools around it
Feelings of closeness, warmth
I stare into others' eyes

I see pain, kindness, joy, agitation, confidence, serenity, wisdom, viscousness

The rush of life is gone

Why aren't all tables round?
Rooms?
Building?
The universe?

FEBRUARY 7, 2021

Man, or Thing

BY HENRY R. KRAUSS

Wrinkled body
Crooked bones
Drooling
Rotten teeth
Diapers
Wheelchair

What story did he/she write?
Savant or Ordinary?

Broken dendrites and synapses?
Smashed brain?
Disturbed DNA, RNA, TRNA?
Senility?
Darkness?
Physical?

OR

Consciousness?
Feelings?
Creativity?
Wisdom?
Imagination?
Ideas?
Energy-Light?
Metaphysical?

FEBRUARY 21, 2021

The Eclipse of G-D

BY HENRY KRAUSS

A little girl, tightly gripping her mother's hand.

Tattered grey coat. Round beaming face. Laughing blue eye. Flaxen hair. Rosy cheeks.

Bitter cold. Separated from mother. Tears welling up, and streaming down her cheeks

A grotesque grey pall lingered over her contorted body. Empty eyes.
Burned in the oven. Tiny body, charred from skull to torso.

Two starving little ones.
Sharing a crust of bread.
Shoulder to shoulder.
Embracing one another.
Kissing and hugging one another, amidst the stench of vomit and feces, which filled their lungs

The Robin

BY HENRY KRAUSS

Bare trees
Grey sky
Raw wind
Chunks of mud, sticks, and grass molded into a circle of cemented leaves.

A robin feeds her chicks,
Hovering-keeping them warm and safe

Why don't some of us learn from nature?

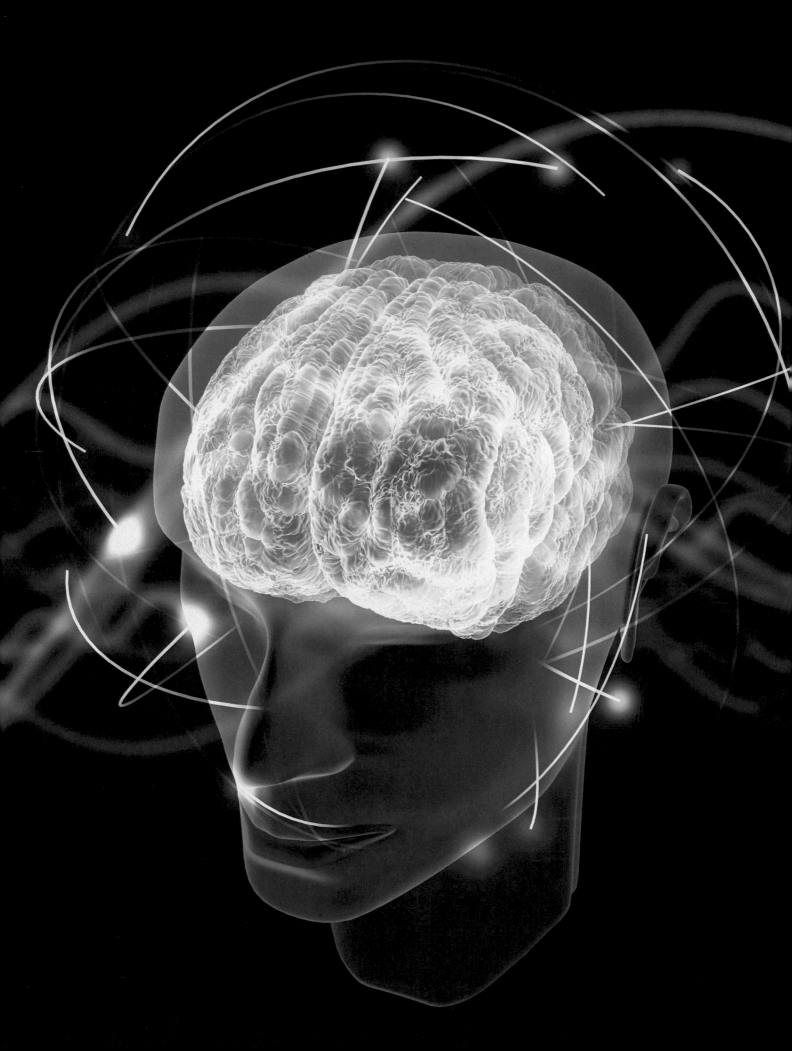

MARCH 10, 2021

Omniscient-Omnipresent

BY HENRY KRAUSS

Energy sparks matter
An enzyme-a cause
Action, not Reaction
Spirit affects an object
Absent it - object decays-implodes, darkness, neglect

Courses through man-through the heart and bloodstream
Microcosmic

Force surrounds the universe-Macrocosmic

Who is behind this POWER?

APRIL 5, 2020

The Rose

BY HENRY KRAUSS

A light, pink sky at dawn, akin to a rose

Stems with sharp thorns

To protect its beauty?

Or

To remind it of its flaws?

We all have what we think as beautiful petals

But

We also have sharp thorns

APRIL 5, 2020

Birds

BY HENRY KRAUSS

Did you ever wonder why birds fly south-in flocks?

Is it instinctive? -free choice? Protection? Or the virtue, character, idiosyncrasy of the leader?

APRIL 5, 2021

My Cancer

BY HENRY KRAUSS

Where did my energy go? I climbed mountains-ran with the wind-climbed the great oak.

Now it's hard to walk, climb steps. I need stamina-vitality.

I sit and can't get up-dizzy-What will rejuvenate me?

My heart pumps, although it feels like the blood is slowly dripping out of me.

Despite the fatigue, I push with grit. I'm optimistic. Tomorrow is another day

APRIL 5, 2021

Outside Looking In

BY HENRY KRAUSS

Deep blue sky
Puffy clouds
Bright sun
Slight breeze
Children dancing, singing, giggling

I'm bleary-eyed, anxious, sad for no reason
A black cloud hovers over me-gloom, "The Black Dogs "as Churchill put it

The happy world passes me by
I'm cold, weep, shiver, anemic

Yet tomorrow is a new day, resurgence

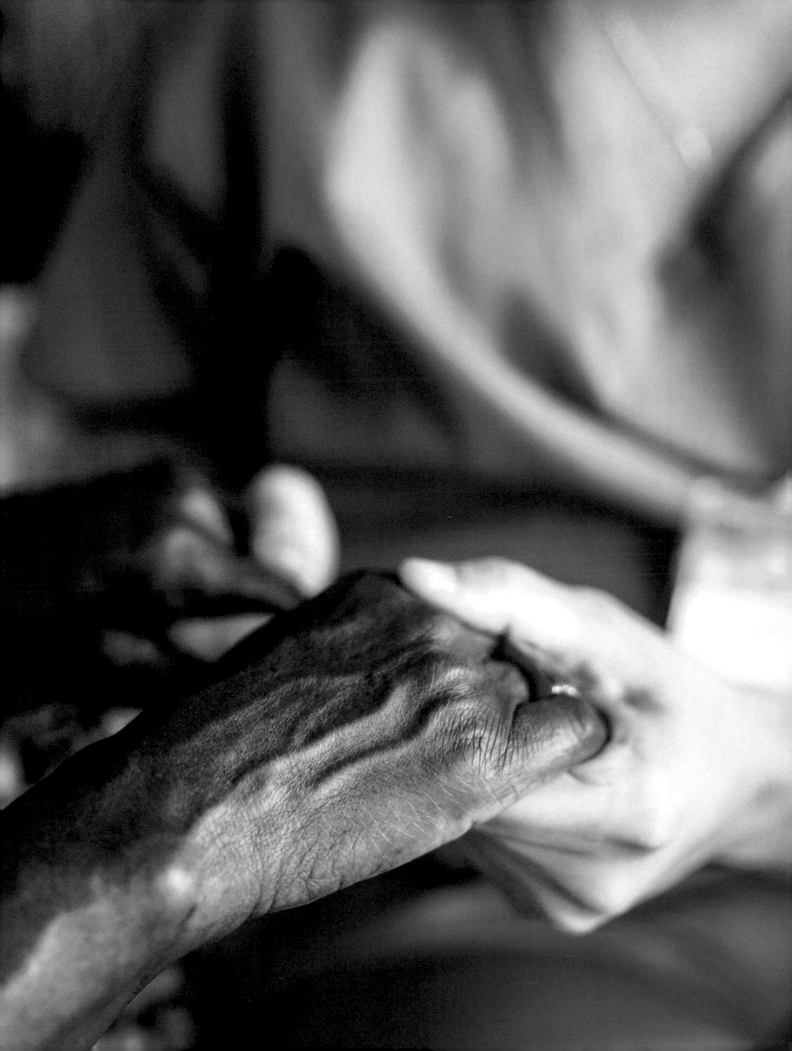

APRIL 5, 2021

The Nurse

BY HENRY KRAUSS

She came on a gray, rainy day-dressed simply -a white coat and colorful shawl
She seemed to be burdened with all she had to carry-sparkling eyes and friendly smile
She was calm, asked many questions about the pictures of my ancestors on the wall.

She had empathy-she was whole
She treated me like a person-a patient, not as a number.

APRIL 6, 2021

Trees

BY HENRY R. KRAUSS

Trees resemble people

Some hang sadly-they break in the wind
A few are crooked -dark and angry, immovable

Others, majestic, imposing, stately, bending in the wind
Many are commonplace, with no distinct features

All are subject to the elements
Their retort is crucial.

APRIL 6, 2021

Monday Morning

BY HENRY R. KRAUSS

I'm dreary-eyed, unfocused, tired

I was up all night thinking about a decision

Finally, I dove into the ocean

The waves engulfed me

I was elated, triumphant.

Who could sleep?

I hit my mark

What Counts?

BY HENRY R. KRAUSS

His face is deeply wrinkled
Bones crooked and broken
Bald, no teeth
Shrunken body

Energetic
Intelligent
Wise
Empathetic
Dynamic
Vigorous
Kindness

How do we view this man?
Past? Present? future? Or ALL?

APRIL 11, 2021

The Hourglass

BY HENRY KRAUSS

I have cancer

The hourglass, though opaque and tiny, is constantly on my mind
It grows, the opaqueness disappears, when I go to my doctor. Depression sets in

I feel things with intensity, that healthy people don't feel- how can they?
Butterflies, birds, trees, mountains, rivers, meadows.

A child writhes in pain, vomits, baldness I also feel the hourglass-extreme pain

I know, that with time and hope the depression will lift. Living life one day at a time, optimistically
with an eye toward joyful projects, will shrink the hourglass and bring the opaqueness back.

Power

BY HENRY R. KRAUSS

What powers electricity, cars, heat, internet, cell phones?
What is behind the power?
What happens when the power shuts down?
What lights up the world?

Generators? power grids? Power plants?

Intelligence, planning, forecasting, testing, invention

Who creates the power plants? The grids? Computers?

Man-the light behind the radiance

And who designed man?

Rain

BY HENRY R. KRAUSS

It trickles
It splatters
It can be soft and warm
It can be raw and mean
It can blow like a cyclone

Damage is directly proportional to its form
Sometimes we walk in a drizzle, sometimes in a thunderstorm, sometimes in a typhoon.
We feel that it will never end

But even a cyclone runs its course
Eventually the sun shimmers-sparkles-glistens

APRIL 15, 2021

The Sullen Girl

BY HENRY R. KRAUSS

She is eleven years old
Her eyes aren't bright, shiny or wide
Her face is inappropriately round
She has an unsightly appearance

She is shy-quiet- to herself
She doesn't seem to have many friends
She seems lonely

She is bright-intuitive-pleasant-courteous
Her soul is caring, thoughtful, gentle, softhearted

People pass her by, as if she's invisible. They don't ask her opinion, her thoughts,
feelings what she perceives. Rather, they engage the "pretty" girls

Still waters run deep.

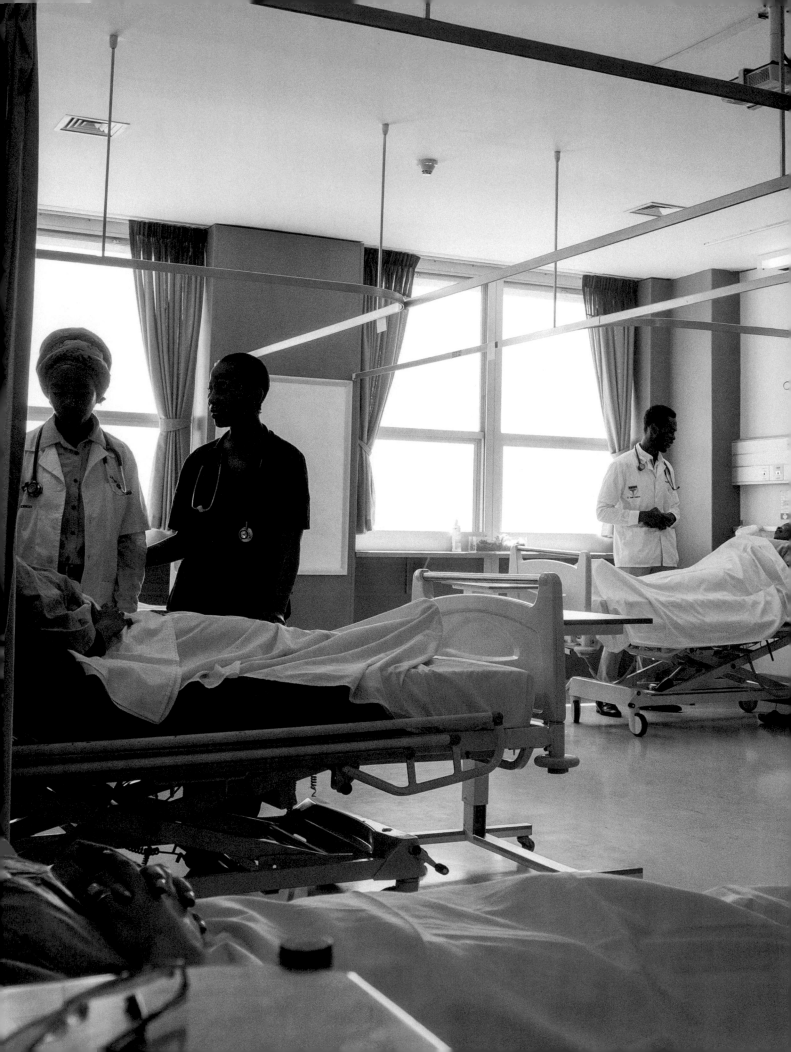

APRIL 16, 2021

In the Eyes of the Beholder

BY HENRY R. KRAUSS

They were in room 5A-5B
Two beds-one near the window, the other closer to the bathroom
There was oxygen over one bed-a blood transfusion machine- two "clickers" to summon
the nurses-blood pressure machines, thermometers-needles and medications

A foul odor of feces and vomit permeated the air. It swallowed you up
The boy in bed 5A was jaunt iced- ematiated-90 lbs.
He had a mouth pan to catch unexpected vomit.
He had blood clots in and on his legs
He had pancreatic cancer

In bed 5B lay a grown man-built like a football player
In fact, he played for "Bama"
He had cancer too-colon cancer
But they caught it early and believed it could be resected

Nevertheless, he was bitter-depressed-angry-afraid-sad-nonfunctional. Will he ever
play again? What about professional ball? What about his finance?

The boy was always smiling-working and playing on his computer, reading
Looking for friends in the hospital-calling friends and relatives to visit-resilient, positive
Although, every once a while a tear trickled down his cheek

He'd look out the window when it was raining and managed to see the blue streaks in the sky.

"It's all in the eyes of the beholder"

APRIL 18, 2021

A Twinkle in his Eye

BY HENRY R. KRAUSS

He was disheveled, collar grey-black
Missing buttons, torn sleeves
Strange odor
Horrid breath
Trousers that reached his calves
Worn-out belt that couldn't contain his bulge
Ranting

People has contempt for him-he was scorned
Insulted
Deprecated

But he had a gleam in his eye-gentle
He overlooked the pain but was thoughtful
The gleam was soft, despite the deprecation

Uncle Al

BY HENRY R. KRAUSS

When we were little, we visited our uncle Al in the Bronx
The trip was endless for us kids

The apartment, built in 1901, was stuffy
It shook when the L passed by
Electricity replaced gassed lights
High ceilings and windows
Furniture from the late 19th century

Gloomy
Paint chipping
Sun silhouetted through the dull grey curtains
Elaborate moldings
Electric fans
Fresh, thick, corned beef sandwiches

Uncle Al rarely went out of his room
When he did, he climbed through the window in his bedroom
He was a lineman, operating radios, behind Nazi lines
He was shellshocked- hospitalized in the Plymouth Psychiatric Clinic

His friend was decapitated by a grenade
Brains, blood, and bones fell on him
The rest of the neck was spurting blood
The encrusted body of his other friend was incinerated, a round,
clump of blackened trunk was the only thing left

He was neither bitter nor angry. He blamed no one, but himself. He was taciturn kindhearted and gentle.

We'd go fishing together, he showed me his photography lab-discussed
his stamp collection -his precious book compendium

We became one. I looked up to him. I adore him still and miss him

APRIL 25, 2021

Microcosm – Macrocosm

BY HENRY R. KRAUSS

I was in a plane
It seemed to be standing still
Tiny cars, like ants sped by on the ground
Their macrocosm was, to me, a microcosm
To the universe above, my macrocosm was a microcosm
We lose our perspective in our "macrocosm"

"Gennie"

BY HENRY R. KRAUSS

She was short-heavy-set
Simple blouse-missing buttons
Torn jeans
Thick glasses
She read in braille
Great-great grandparents were slaves picking cotton in Mississippi

Incisive
Clever
Shrewd

She ran a coffee stand in town hall-to survive
Deep southern, Ebonics accent
Surrounded by Jim Crow and the Klan-all her life
Cousin torched and lynched for looking at a white girl

We became one soul-spirit-essence

Some stole from her
Why do some prey on the weak? Meanness-callousness-malice-spitefulness?

"Nothing is easier than to denounce the evildoer; nothing is more difficult than to understand him.", Fyodor Dostoevsky

APRIL 28, 2021

Quietude

BY HENRY R. KRAUSS

Sometimes life is overwhelming-devastating
Walls shrink in on you- triggering a catatonic state
There are no answers-no apparent remedy
Only we, ourselves can solve the struggle-the discord
So, we go to a tranquil, serene, sacred, place to sort out our thoughts and feelings
The peaceful atmosphere settles us down-the cloud seems to lift
Thinking and feeling are clearer
Sometimes we need quiet places to be alone and think

"I would my life were like a stream," Said her named Emma Jane. "So quiet and so very smooth, So free of every pain. Rebecca of Sunnybrook Farm, by Kate Douglass Wiggins

APRIL 28, 2021

Time

BY HENRY R. KRAUSS

Two trains next to one another
One moves forward
The other simultaneously appears to be moving backward
Is time faster on the forward moving train? Or not?

A plane at 5000 feet. Time appears stationary in the cabin
But to the tiny fast-moving cars below, time is speeding by.
Is time absolute or relative?

Is the age of the universe Creationist, or Cosmological?

JUNE 6, 2021

A Boat in the Sea

BY HENRY KRAUSS

Sizzling lightning
Crackling thunder
Black clouds
Rushing winds
Towering waves
A small boat
Moving up and down with the surging waves
Hopeless
Will it ever end?
Akin to life
Up and down
How do we keep it level?
How do we cope?
Adjust? Especially when we think it will last forever
We are all in boats floating through the ocean of life

JUNE 9, 2021

Pop

BY HENRY KRAUSS

He was reticent. He enjoyed reading and liked to do the Sunday New York Times crossword puzzles in ink. He had common sense and was satisfied with very little. He rarely spoke negatively about anyone. He loved us, but didn't show it physically. He was responsible, loyal, trustworthy. He was a family man, owned a house, and together with mom raised us kids. He was frugal when it came to himself, but in terms of the family, spent whatever was necessary.

He was realistic. Average, was ok, as long as you worked hard and accomplished. He didn't speak of the Depression or WWII.

He said that, unlike the movies, life doesn't always "go happily after ever"

To the Manor Born

BY HENRY KRAUSS

For the few fortunate ones, their lives are set at birth, fortune, fame, breed

For most of us, though, life is tough; money is short, work is arduous, no notoriety, no birth right
But we have free choice.

However, there are the strong few who rise above their station in life-
they use their free choice to find opportunities

Who is stronger?

The one who doesn't have to make choices- the one who is, "To the Manor Born,"

Or the one who is not?

JUNE 9, 2021

Dad

BY HENRY KRAUSS

When we were young, we called our father, "dad", like most kids.

He always smoked a pipe, and the fragrance of cherry wood filled our home.

He picked up the pipe serving in WWII. He had a whole collection. – He even had a long "peace pipe"!

He loved to sit in HIS CHAIR, smoke his "pipe of the day", and read the newspaper. He didn't watch television, he thought it was folly.

He loved Macintosh apples and would buy them by the bushel.

He was born in 1914, had very strict parents-the apple didn't fall far from the tree, and we didn't fall far from HIS tree!

All he had to do was look at you, and you froze

He once returned a roll of cash to the manager of a men's clothing store. It was hidden in a coat pocket-left by another customer

"Veracity is the heart of morality", Thomas Henry Huxley

Aunt Esther

BY HENRY KRAUSS

She was diminutive- frail
Walked with a limp, due to a severe burn sustained in childhood
Liked to wear, white, cardigan sweaters, and,
Wore stockings with black stitches down the back

Spoke four languages
Worked as a chemist-but could also quote Shakespeare

She was dour-serious-disciplined-but intense, durable, resilient
I'll never forget her.